HORIZONS

Poems as Far as the Eye Can See
by **JANE YOLEN**

Photographs by
JASON STEMPLE

Wordsong | Boyds Mills Press

To Joan Hyman and Kent Brown — J. I.

To my biggest fan, my sister, Heidi — J. S.

Text copyright © 2002 by Jane Yolen
Photographs copyright © 2002 by Jason Stemple

Published by Wordsong
Boyds Mills Press, Inc.
A Highlights Company
815 Church Street
Honesdale, Pennsylvania 18431
Printed in China

Publisher Cataloging-in-Publication Data

Yolen, Jane.
Horizons : poems as far as the eye can see / by Jane Yolen ;
photographs by Jason Stemple.—1st ed.
[32]p. : col. photos. ;   cm.
Summary: Poems and photographs depict horizons created by
mountains, deserts, city skylines, bodies of water, and
other natural and man-made areas.
ISBN 1-56397-197-6
1. Nature—Juvenile poetry. 2. Earth—Juvenile poetry.
3. Children's poetry, American. (1. Nature—Poetry.
2. Earth—Poetry. 3. Poetry.) I. Stemple, Jason. II. Title.
811.54 21 2002 CIP AC
2001098539

First edition, 2002
Book designed by Jason Thorne
The text of this book is set in 18-point Dante.

Visit our Web site at www.boydsmillspress.com

Front cover: Canyonlands National Park near Moab, Utah; back cover: the northern Highlands of Scotland; page 1: Everglades National Park, Florida; pages 2-3: Canyonlands National Park; pages 4-5: on the road to Anstruther, Fife, Scotland

CONTENTS

A Note from the Author 4

Sand, Sun, Stone 7

Mirror 8

MoonFall 11

Lake Clouds 13

Horizon with Deer 14

Horizon 16

Sunset Horizons 19

Folly 21

Scottish Beach 22

Study in Yellow and Brown . 25

Coastline 27

One Sheep, One Horizon . . 28

Bass Rock 31

City Skyline 32

A Note from the Author

HORIZON: 1. the line where earth and sky appear to meet
2. the limit of a person's experience or knowledge

The world has millions of horizons, because wherever you look, the sky seems to meet some part of the earth: a meadow, a mountain, a river, a sand dune, a line of houses stretching across the sky.

When my son Jason Stemple began sending me photographs of horizons he had seen, my horizons (experiences) were stretched. I responded to his horizons with poetic insights of my own. They, in turn, stretched his horizons (knowledge).

So we covered both dictionary definitions at once without realizing it.

Eventually, a book happened.

Perhaps these photographs and poems will stretch your horizons, too, till you can see the long line of sky as a curtain rising above the stage, inviting you to a play, a celebration, a moment of understanding.

The sun is an odd period
Over the horizon's long sentence.
I cannot read it.
My tongue stumbles:
Sand, sun, stone.
The desert is a different language
From my own.

northern Arizona

MIRROR

Two horizons, two skies,
The trees meet trunk to trunk.
The word is *reflection*.

If I reflect on the water, I see
Two horizons, two skies,
Yet strangely the world has shrunk.

Two horizons repeat, not divide,
Hands clapping, a water's applause.
What an odd-shaped chunk

Of a world, where sky sees sky.
And no birds can possibly fly.

Whately Reservoir, Whately, Massachusetts

MoonFall

Moon ball,
Moon fall.
Three points if it hits the horizon.

Canyonlands National Park near Moab, Utah

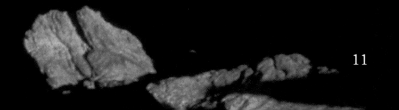

LAKE CLOUDS

See the clouds above the lake,
settling on the horizon
like an old woman's shawl.
Can you hear her muttering,
making her way up to bed?
Her voice sounds exactly
like the water against the shore:
"Time to wash, wash, wash."

Yellowstone Lake, Wyoming

HORIZON WITH DEER

The world tilts,
Sky and earth exchange places.
All that grounds me are four tall trees
And the deer strung along the horizon.

When I am hurt,
I tilt inside like a snow paperweight.
Let me remember then this curve of earth,
The deer strung along the horizon,

To set my gyroscopic heart
Back to the place where love can start.

Crested Butte, Colorado

HORIZON

Just as the thin line
in a long division problem
divides the greater number
by the smaller,
horizon
divides earth and sky.

Gozinta, my mother called division,
explaining to me
the mysteries of math.
But earth does not gozinta sky,
held in place by horizon,
else we would all be flung,
unwilling, into the greater stars.

Everglades National Park, Florida

SUNSET HORIZONS

When the ball of fire
Touches earth,
The mountains will flame.
Nothing but night
Can put it all out,
That perfect fire fighter,
Who comes every time
Without being called.

*double exposure composed of sun and clouds
from the Florida Keys and the mountains and
loch from the northern Highlands of Scotland*

19

FOLLY

FOLLY: a name given to any structure
constructed as a foolish act by the
builder; for example, a belvedere,
a raised turret, a summer house

A foolish act, indeed,
to invent horizon,
that strong divide,
that sliced landscape,
that halved photo,
that jigsawed picture,
that folly of an unbalanced
eye.

Stonehaven War Memorial, in the shape of a folly,
photographed from Dunnottar Castle, northeast Scotland

SCOTTISH BEACH

Each wave a white horizon
Cresting toward shore,
Breaking on the sand.
If all skylines moved this way,
I would be seasick
For the rest of my life.

northern coast of Scotland

STUDY IN YELLOW AND BROWN

Like cut paper,
one mountain lies across another,
a collage of ridges.
Whose hand held the scissors
that trimmed the horizons?
Art, they say, is in the eye,
not the hand, but still
we have to admire the skill that cut
those perfect mountains,
those well-trimmed clouds,
those several studied horizons.

La Garita Mountains, Colorado

COASTLINE

Houses like pearls stretched out
on the string of horizon
along the East Neuk, the neck of Fife.
Come count the jewels,
the oldest hold their shapes best.
See how they complement
the exposed shoulders of the land.

Crail Harbor, Fife, Scotland

One Sheep, One Horizon

Guarding the line,
A crown of horn,
King by design,
Mantled by morn.

Watching his flock,
Standing alone,
His kingdom a rock,
His treasure but stone.

Almont, Colorado

29

BASS ROCK

OK, I know it's a volcanic plug.
I've read about that.
But what would happen if a great hand
came down from the sky,
touched the horizon line,
then pulled the plug?
Would the water of the Firth
whirl down some big Scottish drain,
leaving only the oily sands behind
and some cosmic rubber ducky?

Firth of Forth, Scotland

CITY SKYLINE

Each building
With its evening face
Waits to blast off
Into space.

Overhead
The latest flight
Turns its vapor
Trails to night.

What transporting
Imagery
A sunset skyscape
Offers me.

Charlotte, North Carolina